How Living Things Grow and Change

by Rose Murray

How do sea turtles grow and change?

Living things need food and water.
Some living things can move.
Living things grow and change.

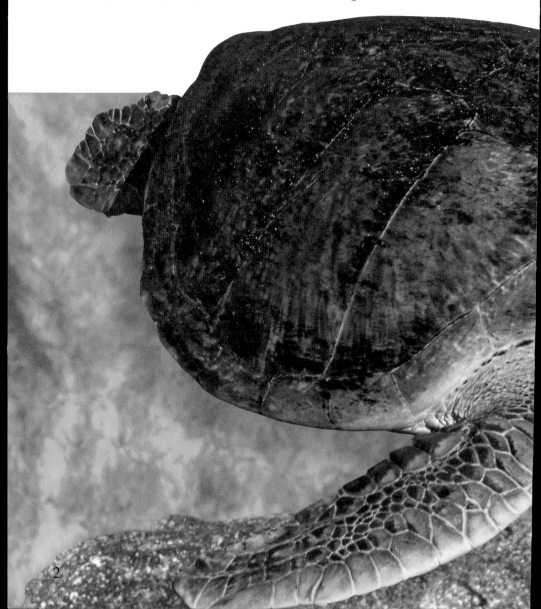

Animals are living things.
Plants are living things.
Some living things can be parents.

Sea Turtle Eggs

A sea turtle is an ocean animal.
It digs a hole in the sand.
It lays eggs in the hole.

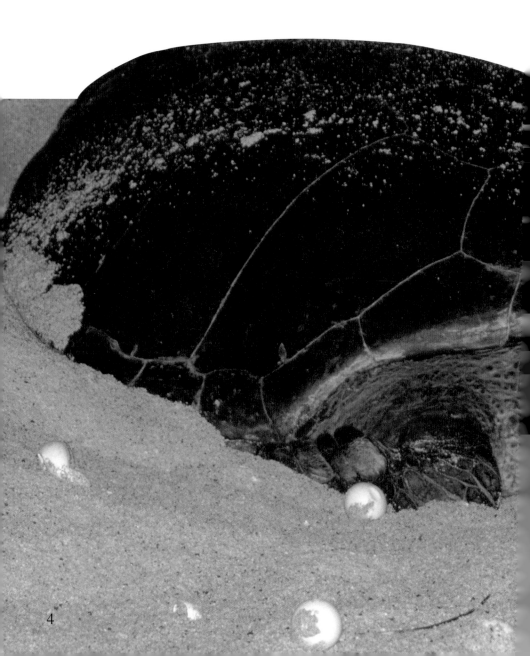

The eggs lie in the sand for two months.
Then they hatch.

Baby turtles have an egg tooth.
They use the egg tooth to get out of the egg.
Later, the tooth falls out.

The Life Cycle of a Sea Turtle

A **life cycle** is the way a living thing grows and changes.
Look at the life cycle of this sea turtle.

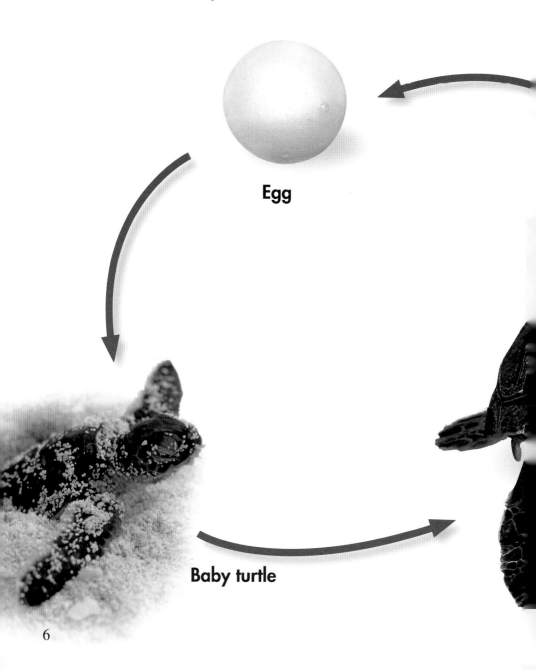

Egg

Baby turtle

The grown-up turtle can lay eggs.
It can start a new life cycle.

Grown-up turtle

What is the life cycle of a dragonfly?

Insects have life cycles.
Insects start as eggs.
Many baby insects are called **nymphs.**
Nymphs look like their parents
without wings.
Nymphs shed their hard skin as they grow.

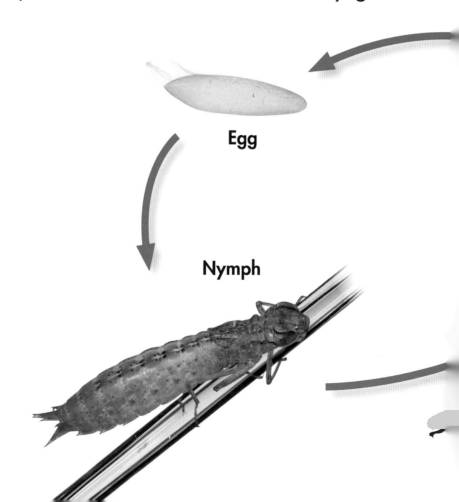

Egg

Nymph

Dragonflies lay eggs in water.
Nymphs come out of the eggs.
Nymphs grow up.
Then they can lay eggs.
Now the life cycle starts again.

Grown-up dragonfly

What is the life cycle of a horse?

A horse is a mammal.
Mammals have a life cycle.
Baby mammals grow in their mothers.
They get milk from their mothers.

A baby horse is called a foal.
It looks like its parents.
When a foal grows up it can have new foals.
Then the life cycle starts again.

How are young animals like their parents?

Baby animals can look like their parents.
They can be the same shape.
They can be the same color.
Baby animals can be different in some
ways too.

All giraffes have spots.
The spots on a grown-up giraffe are dark.
The spots on a baby giraffe are not as dark.

What is the life cycle of a bean plant?

Plants grow from seeds.
A seed is the start of a plant life cycle.
A seed has a cover called a **seed coat.**
The seed coat keeps the seed safe.

A seed has a tiny plant in it.
A seed holds food inside.
The tiny plant needs water and air too.
Then it will **germinate,** or grow.

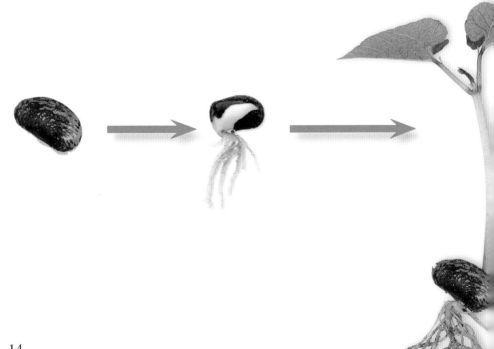

Roots will grow down.
A stem will grow up.
This is called a **seedling.**
A seedling is a small plant.

One day a seedling will be a big plant.
It will grow flowers and seeds.
Then the life cycle will start again.

How are young plants like their parents?

Small plants can look like their parents.
They can be the same color.
They can be the same shape.
They can look different in some ways too.

A young saguaro cactus does not have arms. The cactus starts to grow arms when it is very old.

Small foxgloves do not have flowers.
They grow for two years.
Then they grow flowers.

How do people grow and change?

People change as they grow.
You used to be a baby.
Now you are a child.
You grew tall.
You learned how to talk.
You learned how to read.

One day you will be a teenager.
Then you will be a grown-up.

Grown-ups change too.
The color of their hair may change.

How People Are Different

People can be short or tall.
People can have brown eyes.
People can have blue eyes.
Their hair can be different.
Their skin color can be different.

People in families can look like each other.
People in families can look different from
each other too.

Animals and plants are living things.
At first they are small.
Then they grow bigger.
Animals and plants need food to grow
and change.

Living things can be like their parents.
They can be different.
All living things have life cycles.
All living things grow and change.

Glossary

germinate   to start growing

life cycle   how a living thing grows and changes

nymph   a young insect

seed coat   a hard cover on a seed

seedling   a young plant